ORDINARY HOMESCHOOL DAD

Matthew D. Adams

Edited by Sony Elise

@OrdinaryHomeschoolDad

ISBN-10: 1718950012
ISBN-13: 978-1718950016

DEDICATION

To my amazing wife and children. You make being
an ordinary homeschool dad the best job ever.

CONTENTS

Introduction:

What is an Ordinary Homeschool Dad? 1

Ch. 1: What Makes You So Ordinary? 5

Ch. 2: Pray For Your Homeschooling Family 19

Ch. 3: Support Your Wife 33

Ch. 4: We're Going Places 43

Ch. 5: Teach Apologetics 57

Ch. 6: Family Worship 83

Conclusion 97

Resource List..101

References..105

Introduction

What is an Ordinary Homeschool Dad?

And he will turn the hearts of fathers to their children and the hearts of children to their fathers (Malachi 4:6).

Have you ever been to a homeschool conference? Were you inspired by some great speakers talking about how they are just ordinary dads with the same struggles as you have? They deal with the same behavior problems from the 3-year-old. They have the same frazzled wife who is often crying on their shoulder because homeschooling is so hard. Did you think to yourself, *If they have all these problems and are still doing this, then maybe I can keep doing this too. I can help my wife more. She's not as crazy as I thought ...?* Then you head home and go back to work and not much has really changed. Yes, you try to help the kids out with their schoolwork for a while, but you are tired too. You must get up in the wee hours of the morning and fight traffic. You have this grumpy boss and irritating co-workers. You start to think that these conference speakers might not understand your situation. I mean, they speak at conferences and write books for a living. They don't live in the real world where they work a regular job and have the same routine day in and day out. They are not ordinary dads like you!

Our family loves going to conferences. They are motivating, challenging, inspirational, and helpful. We enjoy the fellowship and try to attend several every year. It was after one of these conferences that I began to think about the differences between our life and that of the speakers I had listened to. Maybe it was the letdown after a big event, but I started to consider the fact that I am just an ordinary guy. Don't get me wrong. Many of the homeschool conference speakers are very helpful, Godly men. However, I don't know of any of these speakers who are just ordinary guys like me. Most of the speakers speak and write books for a living. They are often traveling from city to city and convention to convention. In most ordinary homeschooling families I know, the father works a routine job doing things like engineering, sales, logistics, and information technology; or they perform trades such as auto mechanics, welding, and landscaping. I have not seen a "Joe the plumber" speaking at a conference or writing a book on how to be a good homeschool dad. What if an ordinary guy wrote a book about ordinary homeschool things? Would other ordinary homeschool dads read it? Are there ordinary homeschool dads out there that could use some help from another ordinary homeschool dad? What does "ordinary" mean anyway? Dictionary.com defines "ordinary" as follows:

Ordinary [awr-dn-er-ee] adjective

1. Of no special quality or interest; commonplace; unexceptional

How motivating!

2. Plain or undistinguished

Inspirational!

3. Somewhat inferior or below average; mediocre

Now I am depressed. Who would want to read a book by an unexceptional, undistinguished, below average, mediocre, ordinary dad?

Since you are still reading this, I must thank you for choosing to follow along with this ordinary dad. I hope you find this book practical and helpful on your journey to homeschool your children and bring them up in the discipline and instruction of the Lord. Maybe this is exactly what other ordinary homeschool dads need. I want to help other ordinary dads find a way to be more than just a bystander on the road to train up their children in the way they should go. While I do live a pretty ordinary life, I am blessed to have learned a few things that have been helpful in living out my role as a husband and father in a homeschool family. This book is just one ordinary homeschool dad sharing what has worked in our family.

The first chapter is about my journey as a homeschooling father. If my background does not interest you, skip ahead. This book is intentionally short because I know it is hard for dads to find time to read. While I believe each chapter is important, if you don't read anything else, please read chapters 3 and 5. I believe these chapters will be the most helpful to you. Thank you for reading.

Chapter 1
What Makes You So Ordinary?

Hear, O sons, a father's instruction, and be attentive, that you may gain insight (Proverbs 4:1).

Since I have made the claim that I am just another ordinary guy like you, I thought it would be helpful to give some background on what makes me ordinary. I suppose we are all unique in some way, but I fulfill the basics of an ordinary dad. I work an ordinary job as an engineer for an oil company in Houston, Texas. I fight congested freeways to get to work every morning and sit in a typical office like several hundred other people in my office complex. Up until recently we lived in a typical suburban community. We now live on 14 acres outside of Houston, but I still fight the traffic back into town to go to work every day. We have an above average size family like many homeschooling families. We have been blessed with seven children. I am not a pastor, nor do I have any official ministry position.

I was born in Woodville, Texas in 1976 to Ted and Frances Adams and was the 10th of 11 children. When I tell people I grew up in the woods in a family of 13 people often assume I was

11

homeschooled, but that was not the case. However, my oldest brother and one of my sisters did homeschool their children. Since they are 15 to 20 years older than me, I was around my homeschooled nieces and nephews fairly often, but I still did the typical public-school things. I played for the high school basketball and baseball teams. I went to prom and homecoming dances. I also got in a few fights at school and some other minor mischief. Looking back I am so thankful that God saved me as a child and gave me a heart to follow Him. I did have a desire to please the Lord and, though I strayed from following Him at times, I never made any huge mistakes or got into serious trouble.

I joined the Navy between my junior and senior year of high school, and I assumed that I would follow through with that when I graduated. A few months before graduation, however, my oldest brother offered to let me stay with him and go to the University of Houston. I knew that I was going to be the class valedictorian and have some minor scholarships, so I changed my strategy and got out of the Navy before I was supposed to leave for basic training. My brother took me to the superior officer to plead my case. They were not very happy, but when I told them I had a scholarship and was going to college they let me out.

Moving in with my brother was good for me.

They had much higher standards than I was used to, but I was grateful for a place to stay and I didn't mind following their rules. In fact, after living with them for several months, I realized that something had changed in me. I was much more sensitive to off-color humor and the unbiblical worldview that is typically on television. It struck me hard that I had grown up desensitized by watching a lot of unbiblical ideas. During the time I lived with my brother I began listening to good preaching and going to Bible study. I was beginning to think more deeply about what it means to be a Christian. Probably the most significant thing that happened during that time was meeting a beautiful and mature homeschooled girl who was a couple years older than me and way out of my league. She was the pastor's daughter of the small Bible Church my brother and his family attended. Fortunately, my brother required me to go to church with him. Also, very fortunately, there were not many other guys at this small church. Five years later, not long after I graduated from the University of Houston with a degree in Electrical/Computer Engineering, that first-generation homeschooled girl agreed to marry me. Ruth and I have now been married for 18 years.

Beginning Our Homeschool

Marrying a homeschooled girl meant that, from the beginning, we were going to homeschool our children. Public school was not an option. Since my new wife was homeschooled I knew it would be easy. I just had to go to work and let her do all the schooling and my kids would turn out great, right? Wrong! The first time my wife told me how much we were going to spend on curriculum, I realized that I had better take more interest in what was going on. This has been and continues to be a learning process.

My involvement in the children's education has increased more and more from the time my oldest became school age until now that she is a junior in high school. At first, my wife was pretty much doing everything. She would pick a curriculum and ask me what I thought. I would say, "That looks great." Then she would go to work teaching. The following year, she would show me a new curriculum and ask me what I thought. I would say, "That looks great." Then she would go to work teaching. After a few years of this cycle I began to wonder what I was doing wrong. Why do we have to change curriculum every year? She must not be implementing the curriculum correctly. I also noticed that the more children we had the harder it was for her to teach them. She had infants and toddlers running around her while she was trying to teach, and it wasn't working very well. I often came home to an exasperated wife, and I was getting frustrated. After all, she is the expert. She knows how this is supposed to work and I just need to foot the bill.

Slowly, I started to pay more attention to what the older children were doing. I am an engineer. I could fix this if I jumped in and tweaked things. At that point in time my oldest three were using a curriculum with lots of workbooks. I decided it would help if I took on the oversight of our oldest child's work. I just needed to get all the answer keys and quickly grade her work, and we would be done. I dove in only to become so confused that I was ready to change curriculum.

This oversight that I thought would be easy turned out to be very frustrating and difficult for both my daughter and myself. I would get home in the evening and ask her to show me her work and bring me the answer key. I asked for that because I could never find it. I am still not sure if it was my ignorance of the process or if it was very poorly put together, but it was taking way too much time and effort to keep up with what was going on. It was also hurting my daughter. There was one night in particular that I was trying to grade my daughter's English assignment. She was supposed to diagram sentences. I compared her answers to the answer key and realized she had no idea what she was doing. I was chastising her on not learning how to do it and she was in tears when the realization came to me that I had no idea how to diagram a sentence either. I decided I needed to clear the air with my daughter and take the intensity of the situation down a notch, so I ripped the page out of the workbook, put it my mouth and chewed it up. I think we were both shocked that I did that, and we burst into laughter.

We continued to struggle through and finish off the school year, but the next year we changed curriculum. I started to get much more involved in picking out what they used. Through much discussion, my wife and I decided that her efforts were best spent teaching Biblical worldview, character, and discipleship in the day. She also focuses on the younger children's academics, teaching them to read and to be self-sufficient. I work more with the older children, keeping track of their progress and holding them accountable. This means I need to be able to communicate with them throughout the day while I am at work. Fortunately, I spend most of my day at a computer, so we have set up a system where they will email or text me if they have a problem. I respond as soon as I can so that they can move on. We are currently looking at other online ways for me to keep track of their schoolwork. That is what works best for us. I don't want my evenings to be filled with going over schoolwork. We want to enjoy family time when I am home, instead of spending all evening agonizing over assignments. I used to work for a company that I hated working for and had a very difficult boss. One day a colleague brought me a t-shirt. It had a picture of a pirate and read, "The floggings will continue until morale improves." I remember how I felt when I worked there, and I do not want my children to feel that way when I am at home.

Its What Dads Do

My job working in the oil and gas industry has required me to travel. Sometimes extensively and frequently. I primarily work on subsea system design for offshore projects. Many of the projects I have worked on over the years have been located in other parts of the world. In fact, the only continent I have not been to is Antarctica. I have spent weeks in Singapore testing equipment. I have been asked to leave for Australia as soon as possible with no warning and no idea when I would come home. I have been up and down the west coast of Africa with attempts made to rob or kidnap me. Travel is not a friend of the ordinary homeschool dad, but it is often part of what dads have to do for employment.

One Memorial Day we were taking a family trip to the zoo when my boss called and asked me to fly to St. John's Newfoundland the next day. That turned into four weeks of flying to St. John's every Monday and flying home every Friday. The only reason it stopped was because I already had planned a two-week trip to Egypt where I was to teach a group of Egyptian engineers how to operate the system we had sold them. The day before I was to leave St. John's I got food poisoning and spent the entire night vomiting. My wife was expecting a baby and had learned the sex of the baby that day. She was disappointed that I could not be there for the ultrasound, but she called me to share the exciting news that we were having another girl. I could barely speak I was so sick. The next day I spent the entire flight home curled up in my economy seat praying I would not throw up again. I had burst blood vessels in my eyes and looked terrible. It was a wonder they let me on the plane. My flight to Cairo, Egypt was the next Wednesday. On Monday morning I dragged myself into the office in Houston where I had not been for a month. My boss looked at me and told me to go home. Praise God for small miracles.

Being an ordinary homeschooling dad sometimes takes incredible effort. We must purpose in our hearts to give that effort. In the book of Daniel, we are told how he was taken captive and sent to school in Babylon. He was tempted with eating foods that violated the Old Testament Jewish law. Daniel 1:8 says, **"But Daniel purposed in his heart that he would not defile himself with the portion of the king's delicacies, nor with the wine which he drank; therefore he requested of the chief of the eunuchs that he might not defile himself"** (NKJV). Sometimes we must resolve in our hearts to do what needs to be done, to make the effort even when we do not feel like it.

The one good thing about long flights overseas is that you have a lot of time to read. On one such flight to Singapore I read Voddie Baucham's book *Family Shepherds*. In it he gives a great outline for leading family worship. We had been doing family worship for a while, but it was a bit haphazard and sometimes did not go very well. This book was a great help for me to have better control of our worship. I began right away from my hotel room with my I-pad. Singapore is a 13-hour time difference. Before I would go to bed, while the children were having breakfast, Ruth would set up her computer so that I could see everybody, and I would lead the family in a hymn, Bible reading, and prayer. Leading your family to worship our Savior is one of the most important things we can do as fathers. It is not always easy and often takes much effort to pull everybody together. However, this is something an ordinary dad can do. It requires purpose and resolve, but by God's grace we can do it.

Now I want to address the temptations that are out there for a man when he is traveling. You know what I am talking about. It requires making up your mind beforehand what you will do when you are faced with a particular situation. For me, this typically means that I will not even turn on a TV when I am traveling. I will bring good books to read on apologetics or building a strong family. It requires self-discipline, intentionality, and prayer to avoid the pitfalls.

During the four weeks I spent traveling to Newfoundland I was faced with one of these situations that would have been very easy to just go with the flow. There was a custom by the locals to treat guests to St. John's to a "special" evening. I had heard about the initiation that others had been through, and I was prepared to be confronted with it. However, I did not know how the situation would arise. I was invited to a dinner with the group to a nice restaurant. What I didn't know is that the locals had planned to take me to a strip club and perform their initiation ceremony after the dinner. The ceremony involves filling the mouth of a large fish with vodka and having the inductee drink from the mouth of the fish. After dinner I was told where we were going next and I responded that I would not be participating. This created a very awkward moment on the sidewalk outside the restaurant, but awkward moments are well worth the joy of being able to honestly tell your wife that you stood firm. What has helped me in these situations has been to have open discussion with my wife. I have told her to always ask me how I am holding up to temptation. When I am faced with temptation I think about the fact that she is going to ask me how things went. I know that I am ultimately responsible to God, and I want to be obedient to His Word. I also think about how devastating it would be to my wife and children if I fell into unfaithfulness. I want to be able to tell my sons that I have walked in purity as I exhort them to do likewise. I want them to grow up to be faithful husbands, and that starts with my example. If this has been a struggle for you in the past it is time to start over. Repent and accept God's grace and forgiveness. Purpose in your heart to move on in obedience and faithfulness. **"If we confess our sins, he is faithful and just to forgive us our sins and to cleanse us from all unrighteousness"** (1 John 1:9).

We must also purpose to love our wives. I will spend a later chapter on this, but while I am talking about travel I want to briefly tell you about my first trip. I was sent offshore the Black Sea. This was in October right after the September 11 attacks on the World Trade Center and Pentagon. There was a major scare during this trip. An Israeli airliner was shot down by a Ukrainian test missile. I was flying over Ukraine about two hours from the time of the incident. At that time, I worked for an underwater, remotely operated vehicle (ROV) company and our ROVs were immediately sent to look for the black box from the downed aircraft. This was a very scary time for my wife as she heard on the news about a plane that was shot down in the Black Sea when I was headed that way. This was before smartphones, and I did not even have a cell phone. It took a while for me to contact her to let her know I was ok.

My second trip to the Black Sea was during our second anniversary. I found out about this trip from our answering machine. We had been at church for Wednesday night service. When I got home I checked the machine and it was my boss asking me to come to work with my bags packed the next day. I was somehow able to order flowers to be sent to my wife on our anniversary, but I really wanted to call her. I was on an Italian construction vessel, the Saipem 7000. While walking around on the boat I spotted a pay phone. It even took credit card! When I finally had a spare moment, I rushed to the phone booth and swiped my card. Nothing happened! I kept trying and failing. I was at my wit's end. What was I going to do? I kept praying and asking God to make the phone work. After trying for several minutes an Italian man walked by and ask me what I was doing. I told him it was my anniversary and I really wanted to call my wife. I suppose I touched his Italian sense of romance. He said, "Come with me." He took me to the vessel bridge and told me to use the main satellite phone on the boat. It turned out to be one of the men in charge of the operation. I was able to tell my wife, "Happy anniversary." God does answer prayer. Purposing in our hearts to show love to our wives is what ordinary homeschooling dads must do.

There is no mystery as to what is required of ordinary homeschooling dads. The ordinary things are told to us in Ephesians 6: **"Fathers, do not provoke your children to anger, but bring them up in the discipline and instruction of the Lord."** The points to recognize are: 1) Fathers are the ones being addressed and 2) their training should be of the Lord. The following chapters outline what ordinary dads can do to fulfil this command that we fathers have been given in Scripture. We will start with prayer and end with worship while talking about some practical activities in between. These are things an ordinary dad can do, but we must purpose in our heart to do them.

Chapter 2
Pray For Your Homeschooling Family

Rejoice always, pray without ceasing, give thanks in all circumstances; for this is the will of God in Christ Jesus for you (1 Thessalonians 5:16-18).

Prayer can be an elusive thing. Scripture is full of exhortation to pray, yet most of us find it hard to spend much time in prayer. However, the Word of God has much to say about it. We are told when to pray, what to pray for, how to pray, and where to pray.

- 1 Thessalonians 5:17—**Pray continually** (NIV).

- Luke 6:28—**Bless those who curse you, pray for those who abuse you.**

- Matthew 6:9—**Pray then like this: "Our Father in heaven, hallowed be your name."**

- Matthew 6:6—**But when you pray, go into your room and shut the door and pray to your Father who is in secret.**

These are just a few examples. With so much in the Bible on prayer why do we struggle so much to develop a consistent prayer life? The typical reason is that we lead busy lives, and it is difficult to find the time to commit to praying consistently.

For years I recognized that I did not spend the time in prayer that I should. I wanted to pray more. I started reading books on prayer hoping they would change me. I read the first four books on prayer by E.M. Bounds. I did Bible studies on prayer. I prayed for God to help me find more time to pray. This went on for several years without much change in my life. I remember reading about great men of the faith like Martin Luther who would spend hours in prayer every day. Hudson Taylor would get up at 2:00 a.m. and pray for an hour because he knew it was the only time no one would disturb him. I wanted to have this kind of prayer life but had a hard time figuring out how. After several years of seeking to change my prayer life the Lord did change me. It happened quite suddenly, but in a very practical way.

My wife and I know we must work on our marriage to keep it going strong so that our family can thrive. We have spent much time reading couples' devotionals and watching various speakers on marriage. One thing that has had a significant impact on our marriage has been the ministry of Family Life Today. We have attended several Family Life's Weekend to Remember getaways. On one of these getaways I was perusing the book table, and I saw a little book called *How a Man Prays for His Family* by John W. Yates. I grabbed it, thinking it looked like an easy read. It did turn out to be an easy read and was just the swift kick in the pants that I needed. What he said that I needed to hear was this: "We have to decide once and for all, 'I'm going to be a man of prayer, and I'm going to make the commitment of time.' It's not enough just to ask God to help you become a man of prayer; you've got to do it." [1] Seriously! Get out of bed and do it! I already got up between 5:00 and 5:30 a.m. Do I really need to get up earlier than that? Yes, I do. That night, I set my alarm for 4:15 a.m. The next morning, I got up and had the best time in the Word of God and prayer that I had ever had. It really was as simple as that.

There will be objections to this. Most of us do not get enough sleep as it is, and I am challenging you to get less. Getting up that early can be difficult but there are things I do to make up for the lack of sleep. Some nights I go to sleep early. Sometimes I use my lunch break to take a nap. It is not uncommon for me to walk out to my truck at lunch, lay the seat back, and have a snooze. It can be a hard thing to do, but what greater thing can we do for our family than to cry out to our God for them? We have a mighty God and Savior, Jesus Christ, who holds all things together by His power. Should we not be imploring Him on behalf of our families every chance we get? When we do make this commitment to "just do it" God does something in our hearts. The time becomes most sweet and rewarding.

I keep a small journal of things to pray about for my wife, each of my children, other families and friends, our church, our government, my job, and other things. Not long after I started this, I wrote the following in the cover of my journal as a reminder of why I do this.

Pray Without Ceasing—1 Thessalonians 5:17

The journey to develop a strong prayer life has been long and unaccomplished. I have desired to pray more. I read books on it. I studied it. But, alas, it continued to evade me. Suddenly, out of nowhere, the Lord took hold of my heart. He drug me out of the pit of futility and placed me on this chair in our dining room. In the dark of early morning … in the silence of a sleeping world … my heart began to cry out to my Savior. I have much to pray about. My delight is in these moments with my Lord. May they last forever as my heart pours out in anguish, yet my joy overflows. The words on these pages are my prayers to a great God who chose me before the foundation of the world to bring Him glory. May this sweet time of fellowship prepare me for the journey ahead, and be a record of God's grace and mercy in my life and the life of my precious wife and children. 1-20-2012.

Why Must I Commit to Prayer?

The short answer to the "why" question is that God has commanded us to pray. Hebrews 4:16 tells us, **"Let us then with confidence draw near to the throne of grace, that we may receive mercy and find grace to help in time of need."** Jesus told his disciples, **"Watch and pray that you may not enter into temptation"** (Matthew 26:41).

- What is your greatest concern for your children? Bring it before the throne of grace.

- What is your hardest problem in your marriage? Bring it before the throne of grace.

- What is your biggest struggle in homeschooling? Bring it before the throne of grace.

- What is your toughest struggle at work? Bring it before the throne of grace!

"What causes quarrels and what causes fights among you? Is it not this, that your passions are at war within you? You desire and do not have, so you murder. You covet and cannot obtain, so you fight and quarrel. You do not have, because you do not ask. You ask and do not receive, because you ask wrongly, to spend it on your passions" (James 4:1-3). There is much that could be said about James 4 and the pressure to conform to worldly standards, but I reference this here to make the point that when there are problems in our family, the first place we must go is to God. He is merciful and will answer us. It may not always be in the way we think, but He *will* answer us. One of the greatest benefits is the peace that God will grant us when we are with Him. The best way to calm our fears is to go to Him. **"Do not be anxious about anything, but in everything by prayer and supplication with thanksgiving let your requests be made known to God. And the peace of God, which surpasses all**

understanding, will guard your hearts and your minds in Christ Jesus" (Philippians 4:6-7).

I implore you as an ordinary homeschool father to commit to pray for your family. Find a way. If God has commanded us fathers (which He has) to instruct our children in His ways, we must take time to know Him and His ways. As I mentioned in the first chapter, just like Daniel, we must purpose in our heart to commit to knowing Christ and asking God to direct our steps. Do you want to know God's will for an ordinary homeschool dad? In opening this chapter, I shared 1 Thessalonians 5:16-18. We are explicitly told that God's will is that we pray continually. Romans 12 tells us something similar. **"Do not be conformed to this world, but be transformed by the renewal of your mind, that by testing you may discern what is the will of God, what is good and acceptable and perfect"** (Romans 12:2). To know God's will we must be continually renewing our mind. That is done by spending time in the Word of God and praying to our Savior. The time with Him truly does transform us. It transforms the way we think about our family and how we go about homeschooling.

What to Pray

Keeping a prayer journal has worked best for me. I dedicate a couple of pages to each person in my family. This helps me stay focused and on track. If you are like me, when I bow my head and close my eyes to pray, my mind can begin to wonder and before I know it I am thinking about something other than prayer. I place the name of the family member at the top of a page and write a list of my concerns for this person. I pray through this list. This also gives me a way to keep track of answered prayers. As God answers the things I pray about I put a date beside the item to remind me when God answered that prayer.

Below is a list of items I pray for my wife. The first part I adapted from Todd Wilson's book, *HELP! I'm Married to a Homeschooling Mom*.

1. Strength & endurance

2. Wisdom in discipline

3. Patience

4. Persistence, not to grow weary

5. Calmness & gentleness

6. Discernment & fairness

7. Self-discipline

8. Deeper relationship with God

9. Love in all things

10. Inner peace

11. Creativity & innovation

12. Listening heart

13. Sensitivity to the Holy Spirit

14. Contentment with circumstances

15. Sense of purpose

16. Direction

17. Love of learning & teaching

18. Energy & rest

19. Selflessness

20. Joy [2]

After this list I have a section on her relationship to me. I pray that we would fulfill our God-given roles in marriage. I pray 1 Peter 3:7 and Ephesians 5, that I would live with my wife in an understanding way and that I would love her, honor her, and wash her in the Word. I pray that we would have the time we need together and that we would be best friends. I pray that we would enjoy our marriage and show grace and patience with each other. I have a section on her relationship to the children. I pray that she would see the fruit of her work and that the children would be a blessing to her. I pray that she would have the help that she needs. I also pray for her health and any other concerns that may arise.

For each of my children I have a personal list based on where they are in life. These lists consist of things like their salvation, their walk with Christ, their maturity in Christ, and their love for the Word of God. I may pray for their work ethic and their attitude. If it is a baby, I may have a few things on how they sleep or fussiness. It is good to think about each child specifically and to really know where each child needs prayer. Each list is continually changing. I may scratch something off or add something new as I pray through it each morning.

I keep my prayer journal on a shelf in the kitchen where it is ready for me every morning. I typically have the coffee pot set to brew right before I wake up. This helps me get started. I get my coffee, my Bible, and my prayer journal and sit down at the kitchen table. These are truly special times with my Savior every morning. There are times when I have to move my prayer time to my truck. If I wake up late or have somewhere I need to be earlier than normal I will pray on the road. I plug in my smart phone and listen to the Bible. The good thing is that I have prayed through my journal so much that I have it mostly memorized. I will then pray these things out loud as I drive to work. However, this is not my preference as driving can be a distraction from the ability to truly focus on what I am praying.

Consider how you may adapt these ideas to your own life and family. It is a simple way an ordinary homeschooling dad can transform his prayer life. I pray these tips help you to improve your own prayer life and that you may truly depend on Him as you fulfil the responsibilities of an ordinary homeschool dad.

The Benefits of Prayer

Having our prayers answered is the first thing that may come to mind when we think about how we may profit by praying, but there is much more to be gained when an ordinary homeschool dad starts praying for his family. I previously mentioned the peace that God gives according to Philippians 4 that surpasses all understanding. This is a second benefit. There are also other intangible benefits that we might not expect, but that God grants to us when we are praying.

One example is what happens when a child catches you praying. I have heard stories of great Christians who caught their father praying when they were a child. This gave them great confidence and security knowing their father was up early seeking the Lord on their behalf. It gives them a sense that our faith is something real and that we are not just playing games. When children happen to pop out of their room early in the morning and find Daddy with his Bible, pouring his heart out to God, it has a big impact. They know their daddy truly believes what he has been teaching them about Christ. When you tell them, "I have been praying for you about such and such" they know you really have. I have heard numerous Godly men and women tell of catching their parents praying when they thought no one was awake and the impact it had on the trajectory of their life.

Another thing that bonds a family together is having those prayers answered. We often have our family worship time in the evening around the dinner table. When the Lord has answered a prayer, I use this time to share with the children God's hand in our family. When Daddy says, "You know how we have been praying for such and such? Guess what God has done!" the children get super excited. It is not just about some blessing that has happened to our family. It is about what our great God has done and how He has heard and answered our prayers. Through answered prayer our children can see the acts of our extraordinary God through their ordinary homeschool dad.

One example in our life of an answered prayer came in the form of our little farm. I mentioned that we now live on a 14-acre piece of property. We had put our previous house up for sale and spent over a year with no offers. We found the new place and knew it was exactly what we were looking for, but we needed to sell the old place before making an offer. I must mention that my oldest daughter had been dreaming of having a horse for years. This is something we all had been praying much about. After we had had the house on the market for a while we found out that Ruth was expecting our sixth baby. We started looking at the situation and decided it would not be a good thing to be moving at the same time a baby was due to be born. The baby was due in early August and we made the decision that if we did not have an offer on the house by the end of May we would take it off the market. The last week in May came and I had to fly to Singapore for three weeks. We still did not have an offer. With so much going on we decided to not deal with taking the house off the market until I returned. Right after I left for the airport, the realtor called wanting to have a showing. My pregnant wife reluctantly agreed to show the house but was not really expecting anything to come of it. Of course, this turned out to be the offer we had been waiting for. That meant I had to sign and scan documents and get them sent back from a country that has a 13-hour time difference from our home. Eventually everything was agreed upon, and we were able to buy the house we had prayed for. What's more, the people we bought our new house from asked us if they could leave us their two horses. Our baby was born a week before we closed. We truly have an awesome God who answers prayer, and our children will have their faith strengthened when they see God answering those prayers. Ordinary homeschool dad, pray for your family.

Pray with Your Family

Not only should we pray *for* our family, but we should also pray *with* our family. Praying together as a family should be part of our family worship. Family prayer is an important part of homeschooling. We ordinary homeschool dads are told to bring our children up in the discipline and instruction of the Lord, and part of getting instruction is learning by example. Not only is our children's faith built by hearing our prayers and seeing them answered, but they also learn how to pray by following our example. When the disciples asked Jesus to teach them to pray what did he do? He prayed. He gave them an example.

> **And it came to pass, that, as he was praying in a certain place, when he ceased, one of his disciples said unto him, Lord, teach us to pray, as John also taught his disciples. And he said unto them, When ye pray, say, Our Father which art in heaven, Hallowed be thy name. Thy kingdom come. Thy will be done, as in heaven, so in earth. Give us day by day our daily bread. And forgive us our sins; for we also forgive every one that is indebted to us. And lead us not into temptation; but deliver us from evil** (Luke 11:1-4, KJV).

As the leader of our home we need to give our children an example to follow that they may learn to pray as well.

Additionally, we need to pray with our wives. Praying with your wife is probably the most crucial way to help your wife. When she has struggled all day with the children, it brings her much encouragement to hear her husband calling out to God on her behalf. Praying with your wife builds intimacy with her and draws you close together. There are numerous resources that you can use to help you in this area if you are not praying with her. *Two Hearts Praying as*

One by Dennis and Barbara Rainey is a great book to use as a starting point. Try to always spend a little time in prayer with her before you go to bed at night. In the next chapter, I discuss how you can support and love your wife. Start by praying with her and you will become much more than an ordinary homeschool dad in her eyes.

Praying to Almighty God is such a privilege, and we should make it our aim to spend time with our great God and King every day. Consider what Charles Spurgeon, the prince of preachers, said. "If we should always regard prayer as an entrance into the courts of the royalty of heaven, and if we are to behave ourselves as courtiers in the presence of an illustrious majesty, we are not at a loss to know the right spirit in which to pray." [3]

Chapter 3
Support Your Wife

Husbands, love your wives, as Christ loved the church and gave himself up for her, that he might sanctify her, having cleansed her by the washing of water with the word, so that he might present the church to himself in splendor, without spot or wrinkle or any such thing, that she might be holy and without blemish (Ephesians 5:25-27).

Large families tend to run in homeschool circles and we are no exception. We have five daughters and two sons. There is a lot on a homeschool mama's plate. Trying to figure out high school, middle school, preschool, and a nursing baby schedule can be extremely overwhelming to say the least. Then there is taking care of our home, trying to be a good wife, helping with aging parents, and a host of other activities that often bring my wife to the point of questioning her sanity. Husbands, we need to do everything in our power to make sure the wives God has given us are equipped physically, mentally, and spiritually to handle the homeschool load.

A Heavenly Gift
He who finds a wife finds a good thing and obtains favor from the Lord (Proverbs 18:22).

How often do we forget that our wives are a gift from God? Think about that for a moment. God, the creator of life; the one who spoke and the universe leapt into existence; the Almighty God chose to give you a special gift. Your wife is that special gift from our eternal God and creator.

Peter spoke of this gift in his first epistle. In our culture 1 Peter chapter 3 is often overlooked, shoved off to the side, and even ridiculed, but Peter paints a beautiful picture of the gift God has given us.

> **Likewise, husbands, live with your wives in an understanding way, showing honor to the woman as the weaker vessel, since they are heirs with you of the grace of life, so that your prayers may not be hindered** (1 Peter 3:7).

This language of the woman being a weaker vessel is not at all to be taken as condescending or as a disparaging remark towards women. If you are given an expensive vase, you may place it in a prominent place that would protect it as well show off its beauty and value. With our wives, we want to protect her and let her know how valuable she is to us. Homeschool mamas do so much for the family. They are truly invaluable, and we need to let them know how much they mean to us and acknowledge all that they do to serve our families. They also are valuable by the simple fact that they are persons created in the image of God. Lastly, since they are a gift to us from God, as Proverbs 18:22 states, they are all the more valuable.

When someone we love gives us a gift, that makes the gift all the more valuable to us. If a young child colored a picture for us, we would tell that child how great the gift is and how special it makes us feel to receive such a gift. The picture may be nothing but crayon scribbles that will probably be thrown in the trash later, but because our child gave it to us we will tell them how wonderful it is. It has value to us not because of what it is, but because of how much we love the one who gave it. In the same way, our wives are a precious gift from God. The God who saved us from our sins has given us our wives, and that makes them even more valuable because we love the One who gave our wives to us.

When we think of our wives as something of great value, we will want to protect her. Sometimes that even means protecting her from ourselves. I felt like I had been punched in the gut when I read the following words in Richard D. Phillips's book, *The Masculine Mandate*. "I used to think that if a man came into my house to attack my wife, I would certainly stand up to him. But then I came to realize that the man who enters my house and assaults my wife every day is me, through my anger, my harsh words, my complaints, and my indifference. As a Christian, I came to realize that the man I needed to kill in order to protect my wife is myself as a sinner." [4] Ouch! He is absolutely right! We need to do away with harsh words and anger in our homes and treat our wives with love and gentleness. In doing this we protect her from the one who hurts her more than anybody. Showing understanding, honor, and gentleness is how we treat her as the precious vase, or "weaker vessel," which is a gift from God.

Take the Burden from Her

Homeschool mamas automatically take on all the responsibility of our children's education. They will spend hours researching curriculum, going to conferences, and poring over the shelves in the bookstores. They typically have a great burden to "get it right" when it comes to their children's education. It is a huge task and a huge responsibility. It is easy for an ordinary homeschool dad to just leave it all up to her and not put much thought into what the children are studying. Unfortunately, the wife can get overwhelmed and the children get behind, and then we get angry. This should not be. There are some simple things we can do to help our wives with the academics and other needs in the education of our children.

Curriculum & Oversight

When we only had two or three children curiculum really didn't matter much to me, other than how much it cost. It is fairly easy when you only have small children to keep up with their studies. Unfortunately, if you have a large family, you end up with children at mulitiple ages and it can become overwhelming trying to decide who does what.

As our older children began to enter junior high and high school it was difficult for my wife to keep up with what everybody was doing. Her greatest desire is to focus on Biblical discipleship and Godly character in our children. Matthew 6:33 states, **"But seek first the kingdom of God and his righteousness, and all these things will be added to you."** The good news of the Gospel should be preeminent in the education of our children. She also needs to focus heavily on teaching younger ones to read so that they can become more self-sufficient in the schooling as they get older. Helping your wife figure out curiculum is a great way to free her to focus on what matters most. Picking curiculum goes hand in hand with helping to oversee your children's accademic progress.

When I realized that I needed to be the one overseeing what our homeschoolers accomplished, I also realized I couldn't just pick anything or even use the curiculums my wife had been using. I mentioned in the first chapter how my daughter's English program was not working for either of us. What I needed was something that would not take up all our time in the evenings. That meant I needed to find a way to help them during the day, even while at work. What we ended up with is a Christian curriculum that is computer or web-based. With web-based assignments I can check their progress while I am at work. I can see where they are struggling and help them if necessary. The children can email or text me if they have questions and even send me screen shots of problems they are struggling with. This way I do not have as much to deal with in the evenings, and we can enjoy more family time. Fortunately, my job allows me to do this in small pockets of time or at lunch. If that does not work for you, think about what could work. If you have scheduled breaks during the day, you could touch base with an older child to see how school is going.

It is important to find a curriculum that works with your schedule as a father. An ordinary homeschool dad can figure this out. You just need to talk to your wife about where the children are in various subjects. Chances are your wife already knows what options are available and can give you some ideas. Choose something and work out a plan with your children to keep them accountable. This is something any ordinary homeschool dad can do, and it will be a great relief and encouragement to your wife to have some of the shcooling taken off her plate.

Love Her

Ephesians 5:25 tells us to love our wives as Christ loved the Church. This is sometimes easier said than done. We don't always speak the same language when it comes to what makes us feel loved. Gary Chapman wrote a whole series of books on the five love languages. The key takeaway from those books is that what makes you feel loved may not be what makes your wife feel loved. Has your wife ever presented you with a problem that you knew exactly how to fix? When you told her what to do did she end up more upset than before she asked you the question? Being just an ordianry homeschool dad, I can tell you this has happened to me more than once. The problem very likely is that your wife already knows what she needs to do. She really does not need you to offer a solution. She is tired and frustrated, and really just needs you to listen to her and encourage her. Unfortunately, that is not what our natural response will typically be. We just want to fix it and move on. Understanding her need for support and encouragement is a way we can love our wives. I believe this is why Peter told us to live with our wives in an understanding way. It shows love to our wives.

When the apostle Paul told us to love our wives as Christ loves the Church he specifically tells us how Christ loves the Church. He gave himself up for her. Men, you may not like what I am about to say, but please hear me out. There are things we need to give up for our wives to show them the love and support they need. Most homeschool mamas are at home teaching and training their children all day, everyday. Does she often get a break? When you get home in the evening and on the weekends are you taking the load from her or are you spending the time on your own personal pursuits? Christ gave His life for His bride. How might that apply to our marriage? What sacrifices can we make as husbands for our brides?

Before I leave this topic, please think deeply about the picture painted in Ephesians 5. This is a metaphor Paul is using to describe Jesus Christ's relationship with His bride, the Church. Marriage is a symbol of God's relationship with us. When people look at our marriage do they see Christ? If they do not, they are getting a false picture of Christ's love for His bride. As husbands, we need to take this metaphor seriously as a means of sharing the gospel with a lost world. The gospel is the good news that Jesus Christ, the Son of God, became a man, lived a perfect, sinless life, and died on the cross, taking the punishment that we deserved for violating Almighty God's commands. Because of His mercy we will spend eternity with Him when we repent and put our faith in Him. Our marriage should convey that hope that lies within us as Peter speaks of in 1 Peter 3:15. When others look at our marriage they should ask us, "Where does this hope come from?" Why, sir, do you give up your life for your wife? Why won't you go out with the guys tonight? Why can't we play golf this weekend? Why don't you watch these TV shows? Why didn't you spend all day watching football like the rest of us? Because Christ loved me so much that He gave up His life for me and He asked me to do the same for my wife. Husbands, love your wives as Christ loved the church and gave Himself up for her.

An Understanding Way

Consider First Peter 3:7 again, **"Likewise, husbands, live with your wives in an <u>understanding way</u>, showing honor to the woman as the weaker vessel, since they are heirs with you**

of the grace of life, so that your prayers may not be hindered." I can already hear the objections. "It is impossible to understand my wife. She's irrational. She doesn't make any sense." Trust me, there have been times when looking deeply into the eyes of my precious bride I thought to myself, "I have no clue what you are talking about." I fully understand the inability to understand. Consider again what Peter is saying, "Live with your wives is an understanding way." He is not saying that husbands must understand their wives. He is not asking the impossible! He says to live with our wives in an *understanding way*. That's different.

What is an understanding way? What does it take to show understanding to your wife? As with any act of obedience to our Savior it takes the power of God. Consider how the fruit of the Spirit applies to loving your wife. According to Galatians 5:22-23 the fruit of the Spirit is love, joy, peace, patience, kindness, goodness, faithfulness, gentleness, and self-control. These fruits are all qualities given to us by the Holy Spirit that demonstrate understanding. Since we know that nothing is impossible with God (Luke 1:37) we can do this. Therefore, understanding begins by letting the Spirit of God control us. What wife does not want her husband to be patient, kind, good, faithful, gentle, and self-controlled as well as bring love, joy, and peace to their marriage?

The Song of Solomon gives us some practical examples of a husband displaying romance through his understanding of his bride. In multiple places Solomon uses kind and gentle words with the woman he loves. He compliments her looks. **"Behold, you are beautiful, my love; behold, you are beautiful"** (1:15). He honors her above others. **"As a lily among brambles, so is my love among the young women"** (2:2). He treats her gently. **"His left hand is under my head, and his right hand embraces me!"** He expresses his devotion. **"You have captivated my heart, my sister, my bride; you have captivated my heart with one glance of your eyes, with one jewel of your necklace"** (4:9).

We would do well as Solomon did to pray for wisdom (2 Chronicles 1) as we seek to live with our wives in an understanding way. Ask God to help you, through His Spirit, to be the husband God intended you to be. As we meditate on His Word and seek to bless our wives, we would also do well to remember the warning given in 1 Peter 3:7. If we are not living with our wives in an understanding way, we are told that our prayers could be hindered. We must take that warning seriously and remember it when we are impatient, rude, or unloving towards our wives. **"But I say, walk by the Spirit, and you will not gratify the desires of the flesh"** (Galatians 5:16).

Chapter 4
We've Going Places

Go ye therefore, and teach all nations, baptizing them in the name of the Father, and of the Son, and of the Holy Ghost: Teaching them to observe all things whatsoever I have commanded you: and, lo, I am with you always, even unto the end of the world. Amen (Matthew 28:19-20, KJV).

I have always loved to travel. As a child, we typically took a road trip in the summer. We did not have much money, so that usually meant camping as we went. I loved that part of it and still love to take my children camping. As an adult, I have had the opportunity through my job to travel all over the world. Antarctica is the only continent I have not been on. I enjoy seeing new places, but I especially enjoy taking my family places. We have often coupled vacation with times of learning. For instance, my wife and I have gone to several marriage conferences that were out of state or required a long drive so we spent an extra day or two there to visit museums or see historical or educational sights.

In this chapter, I am going to talk about some of the benefits of taking purposeful trips as a family. I know that it is not always possible to take a family on long trips. It can get expensive, and traveling with small children can be difficult. This is not the key to training children and being a good father, but it can be a supplemental tool when you are able to take advantage of it. The priority is a Deuteronomy 6 home.

> **Hear, O Israel: The Lord our God, the Lord is one. You shall love the Lord your God with all your heart and with all your soul and with all your might. And these words that I command you today shall be on your heart. You shall teach them diligently to your children, and shall talk of them when you sit in your house, and when you walk by the way, and when you lie down, and when you rise. You shall bind them as a sign on your hand, and they shall be as frontlets between your eyes. You shall write them on the doorposts of your house and on your gates** (Deuteronomy 6:4-9).

Go to Conferences

Our family has been to many conferences of various types. As I previously mentioned, my wife and I have been to several marriage conferences over the years. These have been helpful to refresh our marriage and restore our vision. I honestly cannot remember most of what I have learned at any of these getaways, but I do know it gave us opportunity to communicate and reconnect. One of the biggest struggles couples often have is communicating effectively. Conferences can get us to talk about subjects we might not otherwise communicate about on an ordinary day. It helps us to get unrealistic expectations out of the way and connect on a deeper level. I love to see how the stress and tension level in my wife's demeaner drops as we spend time together walking about holding hands, talking, and laughing. It does us a world of good.

One year we attended a conference on South Padre Island, where we spent some time on the beach. We also flew to Pennsylvania where we visited Lancaster County Amish country. We took a trip to North Carolina and were able to visit the Billy Graham Library along with a marriage conference. We have always come back from these trips feeling closer and refreshed.

We have done a ton of homeschool conferences as well. From state conventions, Teach Them Diligently, The Noah Conference, father/son and mother/daughter conferences—we have done just about everything you can think of. These have been great for the children for several reasons. Our children get to meet other likeminded homeschoolers. This encourages them and shows them that there are a lot of other families like ours. Sometimes, there are programs for the children to participate in like drama, choir, or photography. When we tell the children that we are going to a conference they always get excited.

We often have some great experiences outside the conference that bonds our family together. Several years ago, there was a mother/daughter conference in Nashville, Tennessee that my wife wanted to take our oldest daughter to. That trip included visits to the Memphis zoo, a couple days in Gatlinburg, and visiting the attractions in Chattanooga like Ruby Falls, the Incline Railway, and Rock City. The day my wife and daughter were at the conference, the rest of us visited the Hermitage, Andrew Jackson's home.

Another interesting experience also involved a trip to Nashville. We went to the Teach Them Diligently conference there one spring. My little ones were able to attend a Patch the Pirate program and my older two were in a drama program. Unfortunately, we all had a cold on this trip. Even worse, our one-year old son, Nathaniel, got a horrible case of the croup. I ended up taking him to the emergency room in the middle of the night. It was a good thing I did because when we got there we found out that he had a touch of pneumonia. We did not make it back to the hotel until early the next morning. It was a Sunday morning, and we had planned to visit a church in the area, but having been up all night with sick kids we slept in. Things took another interesting turn after this. Our plan was to leave Nashville and drive to Sugarcreek, Ohio to visit Amish country. We were late getting out and had to pick up antibiotics for Nathaniel. While driving northward, we saw a sign advertising Lincoln's birthplace. This sounded like a great historical place to stop for a while. We got turned around, not finding it as easily as we should have, but we eventually made it. When we got out of the car I looked up and Israel Wayne, his sister Sony, and his son were walking towards us. Israel is an author and conference speaker who had been at Teach Them Diligently. He offered to give us a tour of the place since he had been there several times. **"And we know that for those who love God all things work together for good, for those who are called according to his purpose" (Romans 8:28).** Our children could see God's providential plan in orchestrating the event, and we were all highly encouraged.

Another conference that has become very special to us is put on by FORGE Ministries. It takes place in late summer in Kerrville, Texas which is about a four-hour drive from our home. This is a small conference, but we have loved attending because of the many friends and great speakers we get to see. In 2015 we did not make it to FORGE because our seventh child was being born at the time of the conference. Her birth turned out to be one of the most challenging times our family has ever experienced. We went to the hospital to have the baby induced, but my wife ended up with an emergency C-section because of a fibroid that was blocking the birth canal. What's worse is that, while in the hospital, she picked up the superbug Clostridium-Difficile or C-diff. She spent almost a month in the hospital and several days in ICU. It came to the point where the GI doctor set me down and told me they were going to start some new treatments. This included intravenous nutrition, an anti-inflammatory used for Crones disease, and a brand new expensive antibiotic that was specifically designed to treat C-diff. He told me that after he started these treatments one of three things was going to happen. First, the treatments would work, and she would start to recover. Second, the treatments would not work, and they would need to remove her colon within a couple of days. The last possibility was that her colon could rupture at any point and she probably would not survive. I have never felt so helpless and scared in my life. My wife writes in her book *Legacy: Reflections of a Homeschooled, Homeschooling Mama*, "All in all I spent eighteen days in the hospital, and most of that time I was separated from my children and my newborn baby. My body was completely broken, I faced daily pain and suffering, and my heart was torn apart from being separated from Ella Ruth. I do not know when I have ever been so broken physically and emotionally." [5] That particular day was spent running from one thing to another at the hospital, and I didn't even get a chance to eat or drink from breakfast to about 9:00 p.m. that night. When I left the hospital, I must have had an anxiety attack or something related to not nourishing myself. While driving down the freeway I began to lose feeling in my arms and legs. I was already out of town and happened to be approaching a Buc-ees convenient store. I pulled in, ran inside, grabbed a bottle of water, and drank deeply. The numbness subsided, and I drove the rest of the way home. Our good friends Stuart and Dianne were watching our children. When I walked inside I collapsed in Stuart's arms, completely drained physically and emotionally. We will always be indebted to Stuart and Dianne for the help they gave us during this challenging time.

You also must help us by prayer, so that many will give thanks on our behalf for the blessing granted us through the prayers of many (2 Corinthians 11:11).

During this time, the FORGE conference was taking place. One evening, a good friend called me from the conference. He told me that the entire conference had prayed for Ruth and our family. They had literally stopped in the middle of a session and prayed for us. After this call, I sat down on the couch with my son, Gabriel, who was 12 years old at the time. He asked me in a shaky voice, "Daddy, is

Mama going to be ok?" There was only one thing I knew to say. Through tears, I told him, "Gabriel, Mr. Keys just called me and let me know the entire FORGE conference is praying for Mama. We also have people all over the country praying for Mama. I believe God is going to answer those prayers and Mama is going to be ok." Had I not received that call from my friend I do not know how I would have responded to my son, but two years later my wife is doing great and the Lord has completely healed her.

These are just a few examples of the conferences we have attended and the experiences we have had. It is not always easy to pull off going to a conference, but I would encourage you to prayerfully consider how you might incorporate the encouragement of a Biblically focused conference into your family homeschool.

History by Vacation

The older I get and the deeper my faith in Christ grows the more I see God's providence in history. The United States of America is truly a product of the Protestant Reformation of the 16th Century. Unfortunately, history, especially Church history, is often seen as boring and/or irrelevant. I know that I didn't really care a whole lot about history when I was young. That being a common case, one of the best ways to get your children excited about learning history is to go to the places where major historical events took place.

Travel and vacation are a great opportunity to learn history. There are so many great historical places to see in the U.S. alone and if you have the opportunity to visit other continents there are many great places to learn about our past. In 2007 my company sent me to Germany for a couple of months and allowed me to take my family along. We had three children at the time and our oldest was only 6, but my wife and I were determined to learn about some of the history that has taken place in Germany and use the opportunity to include those events in our homeschool. The highlight of the trip was when we made the four-hour drive to Wittenberg, the home of Martin Luther. We were able to visit his home, the school where he taught, and, of course, the door that he nailed his 95 Theses to. Being able to see the location where the Protestant Reformation began was amazing.

While in Germany, we also visited one of the most sobering places I have been—the Bergen-Belsen Concentration camp. Bergen-Belsen happens to be about 30 minutes from the company I worked for at the time. This is the concentration camp where Anne Frank died. Over 70,000 people were slaughtered at Bergen-Belsen, most of them starved to death. Seeing the mass graves and the photos and videos of the liberation in 1945 is very eye opening. While it is not a pleasant part of history, it does remind us how precious freedom is, and how easily it can be lost. 1945 was not all that long ago. This gave us the opportunity to bring some of the history of World War II into our homeschool.

While we may not often get a chance to see Europe or other foreign countries there are many great historical places to visit in the U.S. You could spend weeks on the East Coast learning about the Pilgrims, the Revolutionary War, the Civil War, and on and on. Washington, D.C. alone has much to see and do. As you drive, look for those places that remind you of history. I already mentioned stopping at Lincoln's birthplace. We knew that it might be years before we would travel through Kentucky again, so it was well worth the stop. We live in Texas where there are over 3,000 historical markers all over the state. It can be educational to stop when you see one of these and read about what took place at that location. We also have major landmarks like the Alamo and the San Jacinto Monument. If you look around where you live there are probably many interesting history lessons just waiting to be explored.

Share Your Faith

As Christians, we are called to be a light to the world, sharing the good news of Jesus Christ and the salvation found in His gospel. Traveling as a family can bring many opportunities to share Christ with the world. We often talk with our children before going somewhere as a family about how others will be watching us, and that we need to always be ready to give an answer for the hope that is within us as 1 Peter 3:15 describes. We want to be setting an example of obedience and respect. People really do watch you, especially when you have a large family.

> **But even if you should suffer for righteousness' sake, you will be blessed. Have no fear of them, nor be troubled, but in your hearts honor Christ the Lord as holy, always being prepared to make a defense to anyone who asks you for a reason for the hope that is in you; yet do it with gentleness and respect, having a good conscience, so that, when you are slandered, those who revile your good behavior in Christ may be put to shame. For it is better to suffer for doing good, if that should be God's will, than for doing evil** (1 Peter 3:14-17).

This passage of Scripture is a wonderful place to start a discussion with your children about sharing their faith. It demonstrates that we may not always be looked upon favorably, but we do need to be prepared to share truth with others. It shows us that how we respond is also important. We should not back down from sharing our faith, but we should do it with gentleness and respect because that honors Christ. My children like to hand out tracts when we are out and about, but we talk about the fact that if we have children that have out-of-control behavior it would not reflect the gospel well and could ruin our opportunity to give an answer for our hope. In fact, others will probably not see the hope in us if we are struggling to keep our own family under control. However, if we demonstrate to others that we have the fruit of the Spirit it will more likely give us opportunity to share the good news. **"But the fruit of the Spirit is love, joy, peace, patience, kindness, goodness, faithfulness, gentleness, self-control"** (Galatians 5:22).

Having tracts ready to hand out is a great way to share your faith as you move along. There have been many times we are at a drive-through window, and I get tapped on the shoulder and handed a tract. A small voice will say, "Daddy, give them a tract." That brings a smile to my face. Having tracts readily available is a great way to begin a conversation, but I believe it is even more important to demonstrate that spiritual fruit so that others will want to ask where that hope comes from.

The key points to remember is that we should talk to our children about sharing our faith. Talk to them about setting a good example by demonstrating the fruits of the Spirit. Talk to them about the potential of having to suffer for Christ. Talk to them about being prepared to share that good news of the Gospel and give a defense for their faith. This is where I will pick up in the next chapter, but I want to encourage you here to be intentional about training your children to be mission minded and let the light of Christ shine for others to see when you are out and about as a family.

MATTHEW D. ADAMS

Chapter 5
Teach Apologetics

But in your hearts honor Christ the Lord as holy, always being prepared to make a defense to anyone who asks you for a reason for the hope that is in you; yet do it with gentleness and respect (1 Peter 3:15).

I ended the last chapter encouraging ordinary homeschool dads to lead their family to be mission minded and to make the most of their opportunities to share their faith. We live in a world that has increasingly become more and more antagonistic towards the Christian faith. Unfortunately, most children raised in Christian homes are not taught to defend the Gospel of Jesus Christ. In fact, they are walking away from the faith instead of defending it. In Ken Ham's book, *Already Gone*, he talks about these statistics. "61% of today's young adults who were regular church attendees are now 'spiritually disengaged.' They are not actively attending church, praying, or reading their Bibles." [6] These are young people who grew up in conservative evangelical church-attending homes. Ham makes the point that few young people have been equipped to answer the accusations against Christianity. What his analysis

63

brought to light was that middle school and junior high students already had the seeds of doubt firmly planted in their minds. They are already gone. "We are losing many more people by middle school and many more by high school than we will ever lose in college." [6, p. 32]

In order to counter this massive apostasy the church is facing among young people Ken Ham recommended, and I fully agree, that we teach our children apologetics. What is apologetics? It is not apologizing for our faith. The word actually comes from the Greek word which we translate into the English word "defense" as in 1 Peter 3:15. The late Dr. R.C. Sproul described apologetics like this:

> The task or science of Christian apologetics is primarily concerned with providing an intellectual defense of the truth claims of the faith. The term "apologetics" comes from the Greek word *apologia*, which literally means "a reasoned statement or a verbal defense." To give an apology, then, unlike the more current definition of "I'm sorry," is to defend and argue for a particular point of view." [7]

The Dutch theologian Cornelius Van Til, in his classic work *Christian Apologetics*, defined the word as follows: "Apologetics is the vindication of the Christian philosophy of life against the various forms of the non-Christian philosophy of life." [8] By studying apologetics we equip ourselves to answer the critics.

If you have not been engaged in teaching apologetics to your children already, there is a good chance that they may already be asking themselves some of the questions that need sound, Biblical answers. I would encourage you to have some open communication with your children and find out where they may be struggling with their faith. If you do not have a good answer let them know that you have not studied that area yet, but you will find a Biblically sound answer to their question. Then begin to study and equip yourself. **"Study to shew thyself approved unto God, a workman that needeth not to be ashamed, rightly dividing the word of truth"** (2 Timothy 2:15, KJV).

Where Do We Begin?

There are several areas of apologetics that I believe are vitally important to teach our children. The first is the authority, sufficiency, and inerrancy of Scripture. The Bible contains the source documents for our faith. If we cannot defend the truth that the Bible is the Word of God, everything else can be called into question. The second topic that should be taught is Church history. There is a lot of information out there designed to discredit Christianity based on the past. An accurate understanding of Church history will allow you to quickly dismiss the lies and half-truths that are often presented as fact. The third area is Biblical creation. The theory of evolution is taught as fact almost everywhere, yet with a little logic you can find some big holes in this theory. Fortunately, we have some great resources today to equip children to defend their faith against those who want to destroy Christianity by denying the Creator.

Before I examine some of the specifics regarding each of these three areas, I want to briefly discuss a couple of apologetic methods that should be distinguished between. There is often a debate among apologists (men whose ministry is in apologetics) over which method is best. The two methods are evidential and presuppositional. The evidential method focuses primarily on the cold hard facts for demonstrating truth. An example of this method would be Lee Strobel's books *The Case for Christ* and *The Case for Creation*. Lee became a Christian after examining the evidence for the resurrection of Jesus Christ. "What's more, my journalistic skepticism toward the supernatural had melted in light of the breathtaking historical evidence that the resurrection of Jesus was a real, historical event." [9]

The presuppositional method is different in that it first seeks to determine the presuppositions of the unbeliever then demonstrate that their presupposition utilizes a false premise or leads to a logical fallacy. A great book utilizing this method is Dr. Jason Lisle's book *The Ultimate Proof of Creation.* "Presuppositions must be assumed before we can investigate other things. For example, laws of logic are a presupposition. I must assume that such laws exist before I can begin to reason." [10] I admit that the presuppositional method can, at first, seem a bit esoteric, but once you read some of the presuppositional arguments you will see that it can be a very powerful tool that is not easily argued against. We must remember that as a Christian we have presuppositions too. Foremost is that we presuppose that the Bible is truly God's inerrant Word. We base many of our arguments on the fact that the Bible says it, so it is, in fact, true. We admit this whereas the unbeliever will often not admit to having presuppositions that cause them to come to their conclusions.

Before moving on, I want to clarify that presuppositional apologetics does not disregard evidence. There is much evidence that demonstrates that the Bible is truly the Word of God, that God has providentially acted in history, and that we are here as the result of the purposes of a divine Creator. However, the unbelieving heart will always find ways to excuse away the evidence. When an unbelieving presupposition has been demonstrated, the evidence can then be utilized to reinforce the argument. When I read *The Case for Christ* in my early 20s, I was thrilled to have the evidence that reinforced my faith in Christ. My hope and prayer is that an ordinary homeschool dad and his children would study some of these facts and get excited about their faith and the God who loves them and gave Himself for them. **"I have been crucified with Christ; it is no longer I who live, but Christ lives in me; and the life which I now live in the flesh I live by faith in the Son of God, who loved me and gave Himself for me"** (Galatians 2:20, NKJV).

The Word of God
Sanctify them by Your truth. Your word is truth (John 17:17, NKJV).

Teaching your children that they can trust the Bible is the most important truth that you can teach them. Let me repeat that. The most important truth you can teach your children is that they can trust the Word of God. The Christian faith is based on the 66 books of the Bible. This is what we call the canon of Scripture. You might push back on me and say that we really just need to teach them the gospel and that faith in Jesus Christ is what saves, not faith in the Bible. My first response to this is John 1:1: **"In the beginning was the Word, and the Word was with God, and the Word was God."** John goes on to reveal to us that the Word he is speaking of here is Jesus. **"He was in the world, and the world was made through Him, and the world did not know**

Him. He came to His own, and His own did not receive Him. But as many as received Him, to them He gave the right to become children of God, to those who believe in His name: who were born, not of blood, nor of the will of the flesh, nor of the will of man, but of God" (John 1:10-13). We are saved by knowing the Word of God which reveals to us who Jesus is and how we are saved. If our children begin to doubt any part of the Scriptures they will begin to question the authenticity and authority of Jesus as well. If we cannot trust the Bible in Genesis 1, then why should we trust the Bible when it teaches us about Christ? We must teach our children to trust the authority, sufficiency, and inerrancy of Scripture.

There are several methods critics use to try to undermine the Bible. I will briefly address the areas, but I will provide a list of resources that can be used with your children to crush those questions and help build a rock-solid faith in the Scriptures. First, the historicity of the Bible is questioned. You might hear someone say that the Bible is just copies of copies of copies and because of that there is no way we can know what was originally written. The second accusation is that we don't really know what books should be in the Bible. After all, the Roman Catholic Bible has books that are not in the Protestant's Bible. There is no way we can know if some books are missing or if the books we have should really be in there. Lastly, you might hear someone say that the Bible is full of contradictions. There is no way we can trust a book that isn't consistent. If it is full of error, it cannot be from God. Do these kinds of criticisms sound familiar? These kinds of accusations are all over the internet so do not be surprised if your children have seen or heard some of these. We must have good answers to these questions and equip our children to counter them.

Did copying manuscripts cause us to lose the originals?

The study of ancient manuscripts and how we got the Bible we have today is called textual criticism. We have almost 6,000 ancient, hand-written, Greek manuscripts of the New Testament, either in part or in full. By examining these texts, we can be extremely confident that we know what was originally written. The transmission of the manuscripts was not like the phone game where every time it passed from one to another it changed a little until now we have something completely different than what was original. Even when secular textual critics are asked they will tell you that the information we have today has not changed significantly. For an example, you can search YouTube and find the debate between Dr. James R. White and Dr. Bart Ehrman. The testimony of Christ's crucifixion and resurrection is as accurately told in the Bible we have today as it was when Matthew, Mark, Luke, and John wrote their gospels.

Dr. White has recorded many presentations of the reliability of Scripture. I encourage you to look these up on the Alpha Omega Ministries YouTube channel or podcast.

Probably the biggest complaint about the ancient manuscripts is that there are thousands and thousands of variants. A variant is a difference between two hand-written texts. Dr. White says, "When people speak of huge numbers of variants, here is what they are referring to: one manuscript with a unique spelling of a word at one point creates a variant over against all other manuscripts." [11] It is true that there are somewhere around 400,000 textual variants. However, that number can be misleading if you do not understand what those variants represent. "While the idea of having no variants may sound great, variants actually are a natural byproduct of having lots and lots of handwritten manuscripts. And the more manuscripts you have, the better, as far as making sure what you have today accurately reflects what was originally written." [11, p. 64] Dr. White goes on to point out that even liberal textual critics agree that 99 percent of the variations are irrelevant when it comes to properly translating the Greek texts. The vast majority of these variations can be attributed to differences in spelling and word order which is commonly irrelevant in the Greek language. When a variant does have meaning it is often the case that there is a logical explanation such as the *homoeo-teleuton* or "similar ending." This is where a scribe was copying a text but skipped a line because when his eyes went back to the original he saw a different word that had a similar ending as where he originally left off. Dr. White concludes, "A very small percentage of the overall New Testament text is directly impacted by textual variants in the manuscript tradition that are both relevant to the meaning and difficult to decide with certainty." [11, p. 66] I encourage you to read his books *The King James Only Controversy* and *Scripture Alone: Exploring the Bible's Accuracy, Authority, and Authenticity* for an in-depth look into the trustworthiness of Scripture.

How do we know that the Bible contains the right books?

Several years ago, Dan Brown published a book which was later made into a movie called *The Da Vinci Code*. This book called into question what we know about Jesus by introducing the general public to what scholars call the Gnostic Gospels. The Gnostics denied the deity of Christ and other essential Christian doctrine. They claimed to have special knowledge which is where the word "gnostic" comes from. It seems like every Easter or Christmas a newspaper will publish an article on "The Lost Books of the Bible," where they will rehash information about works such as *The Gospel of Thomas* or the *Epistle of Barnabas*. There are a number of these gnostic works which scholars have known about for many years. They were written in the second century and have always been rejected by the church. When you read the works of Irenaeus (c. 180), you see that he clearly rejected gnostic assertions. Saint Irenaeus of Lyons was a student of Polycarp who was a student of the Apostle John. "Irenaeus stands out as the most important Church father of the 2nd century. This is because he wrote against the Gnostics a lengthy book usually known as Against Heresies." [12] Irenaeus called out specific Gnostic leaders and condemned their claim to special knowledge. "Neither Valentinus, nor Marcion, nor Saturninus, nor Basilides nor angels, archangels, principalities, nor powers have this knowledge." [13] It is fascinating to read Irenaeus and see how he was refuting heresies in the second century that still exist in various forms today. He continually went back to the writings of the apostles and demonstrated that their teaching was unbiblical.

If you would like to be thoroughly entertained (tongue in cheek), I encourage you to read some of the Gnostic Gospels. To give my honest opinion, they are just plain weird! They are not at all like the Holy Scriptures. They tend to not have a clear train of thought or they tell stories that are totally unbelievable. Consider this excerpt from The Infancy Gospel of Thomas when Jesus was supposedly five years old.

After that again he went through the village, and a child ran and dashed against his shoulder. And Jesus was provoked and said unto him: Thou shalt not finish thy course. And immediately he fell down and died. But certain when they saw what was done said: Whence was this young child born, for that every word of his is an accomplished work? And the parents of him that was dead came unto Joseph, and blamed him, saying: Thou that hast such a child canst not dwell with us in the village: or do thou teach him to bless and not to curse: for he slayeth our children. [14]

What? This is obviously not the Jesus of the Bible.

It should be fairly obvious that the Gnostic Gospels are not part of the Scripture, but what about the Apocrypha? Is there a reason that Protestants have rejected the Apocrypha, but Roman Catholics include it? I cannot go into all the reasons why the Catholic church accepts it, but I do want to touch briefly on why Protestants do not. We must understand that the Jews in the time before Christ knew what books they accepted as the Word of God. They had laid up in the temple the books of the Old Testament. However, the Apocrypha was not part of these sacred Jewish writings. Dr. Michael J. Kruger states, "In the first few centuries of the church we have good evidence that the dominant position (though not the only position) was an acceptance of the Jewish Old Testament canon and not the Apocrypha. This would include church fathers like Melito of Sardis, Origen, Eusebius, Athanasius, Cyril of Jerusalem, Epiphaniaus, Hilary of Poitiers, Gregory of Nazianzus, Rufinus, and Jerome." [15]

Dr. Kruger gives a beautiful explanation for why we can trust that we have the right books in our Bible in his book *Canon Revisited: Establishing the Origins and Authority of the New Testament Books*. I must quote these three points in full so as not to misrepresent him.

- Providential exposure. We trust in the providence of God to expose the Church to the books it is to receive as canonical. How can the Church recognize books it does not have? Thus, "our" model, by definition, does not address "lost" apostolic books.

- Attributes of canonicity. The Scriptures indicate that there are three attributes that all canonical books have: (1) divine qualities (canonical books bear the "marks" of divinity), (2) corporate reception (canonical books are recognized by the Church as a whole), and (3) apostolic origins (canonical books are the result of the redemptive-historical activity of the apostles.).

- Internal testimony of the Holy Spirit. Because of the noetic effects of sin, the natural man cannot reliably recognize these attributes of canonicity. Thus, we need the internal testimony of the Holy Spirit. The internal testimony is not private revelation that tells us which books belong in the canon, but it is the Spirit opening our eyes to the truth of these attributes and producing belief that these books are from God. [15, p. 290]

In this very detailed book Kruger gives lengthy and convincing justification for the Church coming to the right conclusion on which books to include. In his conclusion he states, "When all the dust had settled, the church had reached an impressive degree of unity about which books it recognized as speaking with the voice of its Master." [15, p. 287]

Is the Bible full of contradictions?

When I was working on my MBA the Mel Gibson movie *The Pasion of the Christ* had just come out. My instructor for Business Law stated one day, "I am not a Bible scholar, but the problem I see with this movie is that it can't stick to the gospels because they contradict one another." I immediately pushed back on this statement and told him that there may be some apparent contradictions in the gospels, but they can be logically explained. He quickly changed the subject. On my final exam the last question was,

"What did you like or dislike about this class?" It was a take-home exam which gave me the perfect opportunity to address his concerns. I quoted Dr. R.C. Sproul explaining the law of noncontradiction and demonstrated a few places where these apparent contradictions were not contradictions at all. I submitted the paper and prayed for mercy. When I received my score, I had made an A on the exam!

It is extremely common to hear people pointing out all these contradictions found in the Bible. The internet is full of websites rattling off lists of contradictions you can find in Scripture, but are they truly contradictions? I am so thankful for Dr. Jason Lisle's book *Keeping Faith in an Age of Reason: Refuting Alleged Bible Contradictions*. He goes through 420 alleged contradictions and demonstrates how they are resolved. "When we actually bother to check, we find that not one of the hundreds of listed examples is genuinely contradictory at all. In most cases, it is clear that the critic has simply not read the text carefully or in context." [16] I highly encourage you to get a copy of this book and read it to your children. It will be fun and faith building to see each one of these accusations dismantled.

The example I used on my final exam was regarding the number of angels at the tomb. If one gospel mentions one angel and another gospel mentions two, it does not mean that there is a contradiction. If there were 2 then there was 1. If one of the gospels had said there was one and only one angel at the tomb and the other said that there were definitely two angels there, then we would have a problem. However, in this case, we simply have one gospel giving a bit more information than the other. It is not a contradiction. It is common in the four gospels that one author will give a detailed record of an event while another will telescope the same event and give much less information. They are simply corroborating that the events really happened.

Church History

People often find history dry and boring, but please believe me that Church history can be extremely exciting. When you examine the record and see God's hand in directing the Church, you will find that Church critics can easily be refuted by knowing a little history. It can become extremely exciting.

Much like the previous section, there is a lot of bad information on the internet regarding the Church in previous centuries. There is often a lot of conflating actions of the true Church with actions that took place in the name of the Church. The good news is that if you do a little reading from early Church fathers and Christians throughout the centuries a lot of these false criticisms can be dispelled. I have recently been reading to my children

Daily Reading: The Early Church Fathers by Dr. Nick Needham. I am amazed as I read through these short daily passages by the refutation of internet critics.

One of the accusations that is often thrown out there is that the Church didn't really believe Jesus was God until the Council of Nicaea in A.D. 325. The first question I would respond with if facing this accusation is, Have you read the Nicaean documents? Chances are they have not. The second question I would ask is, Have you read Irenaeus? Again, it is very unlikely that they have. It does not take much reading from Irenaeus to see that he clearly believed in the doctrine of the Trinity; that the Father, the Son, and the Holy Spirit are three distinct persons that make up the one true and living God. "He was scorned by the people, and humbled Himself to the point of death. On the other hand, He is the holy Lord, the Wonderful counsellor, the Beautiful in appearance, the Mighty God, coming on the clouds as Judge of all humanity! All these things the scriptures have prophetically spoken of Christ." [13, p. Feb 13] This is only one of many statements Irenaeus makes in regard to the deity of Jesus Christ, and he wrote these things circa A.D. 180.

For a Biblically sound, in-depth review of Church history Dr. Needham has also written a 4-volume set called *2000 Years of Christ's Power.* He is working on the fifth book in the set. It is worth having these books for at least a reference source and your children might enjoy reading them in order to get a great foundation in Church history.

It has become a tradition in our family that every October 31st we invite several families over to celebrate Reformation Day. October 31, 1517 is the day that Martin Luther nailed his *95 Theses* to the church door in Wittenberg, Germany and started the Protestant Reformation. My children require me to dress in a monk's costume and act out a short skit of Martin Luther. This has become one of our favorite events of the year, and my older children spend a lot of time preparing games and activities that point us back to the people and circumstances of the Reformation. We have a lot of fun putting this on, but more importantly my children take an interest in the events of history that have shaped the Church today. Consider how you too might make history fun and interesting for your children as you teach them of God's sovereign hand in the history of Christ's Church.

Teach Creation

Creation science is, by and large, disregarded in academia and, sadly, many churches have handed over the teachings on origins to the secular humanists. I am firmly convinced that believing in the six literal days of creation as taught in the Bible is paramount for children to retain a Biblical worldview.

Why is it so important? After all, there are many Christians who have come up with ways of getting around young earth creationism and believe that billions of years is just a given. It is important because once you doubt what is taught in Genesis 1, it is easy to doubt what is taught in John 1. If you undermine the creation story of Genesis, you undermine your faith in God's Word, which leads to undermining your faith in Jesus Christ.

I have already emphasized the importance of teaching children to trust the Bible. Understanding our origin goes hand in hand with trusting the Bible. If it seems like a hard task to teach Biblical creationism, I have some good news. There is a vast amount of scientific information available today that supports the Biblical account of creation. There is also a lot of twisting information by evolutionists to fit their presuppositions. Dr. Jobe Martin chronicles his journey from teaching evolution at the university to believing in Biblical creation in his book *The Evolution of a Creationist*. Dr. Martin was challenged by two of his students to defend his position.

> That seemed to be a fairly easy job since I was convinced that huge volumes of factual scientific evidence proved evolution (over billions of years) to be true. By 1972, this professor's stomach was churning with frustration! The evidence for an old universe

promoted as proven fact by evolutionists was nowhere to be found." [17]

Dr. Martin goes on to document many scientific facts that support intelligent design and young earth creationism. His book is a fun read for the family as it documents the design of some extremely fascinating animals that could not possibly have evolved. He also points out many of the assumptions that evolution is based on and how these presuppositions are based not on fact, but on their anti-Christian worldview. Evolutionists are sometimes honest enough to admit the lack of evidence. In reviewing a book by Carl Sagan, Harvard professor of biology, Richard Lewontin, wrote the following:

> Our willingness to accept scientific claims that are against common sense is the key to an understanding of the real struggle between science and the supernatural. We take the side of science *in spite* of the patent absurdity of some of its constructs, *in spite* of its failure to fulfill many of its extravagant promises of health and life, *in spite* of the tolerance of the scientific community for unsubstantiated just-so stories, because we have a prior commitment, a commitment to materialism. It is not that the methods and institutions of science somehow compel us to accept a

material explanation of the phenomenal world, but, on the contrary, that we are forced by our *a priori* adherence to material causes to create an apparatus of investigation and a set of concepts that produce material explanations, no matter how counter-intuitive, no matter how mystifying to the uninitiated. Moreover, that materialism is absolute, for we cannot allow a Divine Foot in the door. The eminent Kant scholar Lewis Beck used to say that anyone who could believe in God could believe in anything. To appeal to an omnipotent deity is to allow that at any moment the regularities of nature may be ruptured, that miracles may happen. [18]

This tells us exactly what the evolutionist is committed to. His or her presuppositions will not allow for a supernatural Creator no matter what the evidence tells them.

The fact of the matter is there is not a reasonable explanation for life to exist apart from a supernatural Creator. We know this Creator as Jesus Christ. **"In the beginning was the Word, and the Word was with God, and the Word was God. He was in the beginning with God. All things were made through him, and without him was not anything made that was made"** (John 1:1-3). As Dr. Jobe Martin states, "For nearly 150 years, some of the most brilliant scientists in the world have attempted to convert non-living chemicals into some form of reproducible life. No one has done it." [17, p. 48]

Organizations such as the Institute for Creation Research (ICR), Answers in Genesis (AIG), and the Biblical Science Institute (BSI) have produced some outstanding works in creation science. There are many books and articles outlining work that has been done to advance science from a young earth creationist's perspective. Just to highlight a few bits of information that reflect a young earth and a worldwide flood would be: soft tissues found in dinosaur bones, marine fossils found in landlocked areas such as Kansas, the incredible complexity and design features obvious in the Bombardier Beetle, the lack of transitional forms in the fossil record, and the results of what the advancements in genetics are providing. There is not space enough in this book to go into details in all these areas, but I want to briefly look at the last point on genetics.

Dr. Nathaniel T. Jeanson, who holds a Ph.D. in cell and developmental Biology from Harvard University, has written a fascinating book on genetics entitled, *Replacing Darwin—The New Origin of Species*. Without quoting all the math involved, Dr. Jeanson provides interesting information on genetic calculations that support the young earth model by an examination of human mtDNA. "At a mutation rate of one base pair per 76 to 419 years, a minimum of 21,480 mtDNA differences and a maximum of 447,368 mtDNA differences would arise. Today, only 1,483 mtDNA differences separate these two species. The evolutionary timescale predicts mtDNA differences far in excess of what is observed." [19] He says, "The 6,000-year timescale makes even more penetrating predictions." [19, p. 188] Essentially, what Dr. Jeanson points out is that genetic mutation rates can be calculated, and predictions can be made based on these calculations. However, assumptions must be made about the time of origin. If you assume humans began on earth around 6,000 years ago, we can predict with accuracy the amount of genetic mutation we are currently able to observe in today's humans.

Dr. Jeanson challenges evolutionists to use the scientific method to make predictions and then test those predictions. This is something creationists are often discredited for, because we can't test for the existence of God, supernatural creation, or a global flood. However, the young earth model fits the genetic predictions.

> Curiously, the human mtDNA data that we've just discussed fits a model that many have previously discounted. In a previous section I discussed the YEC (Young Earth Creationists) geologists and astronomers who hold to a 6,000-year timescale for the earth

and universe. Predicting mtDNA differences for *Homo* individuals over 6,000 years exactly captures both the average mtDNA differences among non-Africans and among Africans. [19, p. 185]

Dr. Jobe Martin has it right when he states, "Their studied opinion is that macroevolution is beyond the range of 'testable hypothesis.' In other words, it is not able to be proven factually true with the scientific method." [17, p. 81]

Love Apologetics

I was in junior high when a man came to our church and presented some facts from a young earth creationist's perspective. That presentation ignited a spark in me for studying creation and eventually other areas of apologetics. I encourage you to get excited about apologetics as well and start teaching your children that we can trust the Word of God from the beginning to the end. It is imperative that your children are equipped with information to protect them from the onslaught of secular humanist attack they will most likely be faced with some day if not already. I leave this chapter with one final quote from Ken Ham as a reminder of what we are up against.

Unless the facts behind the Christian faith are clearly and convincingly communicated in a way that students can learn and remember, their faith will not stand the assault of doubt from the world. It's not enough to just tell students, "Believe in Jesus!" Faith that is not founded on fact will ultimately falter in the storm of secularism that our students face every day. [6, p. 49]

MATTHEW D. ADAMS

Chapter 6
Family Worship

I have no greater joy than to hear that my children walk in truth (3 John 1:4, KJV).

William Wilberforce, the politician best known for ending the slave trade in England, wrote of teaching children:

> If you are careful and considerate, you will be alarmed that so many parents take for granted the formative years when young children can be influenced and shaped. They seem to think that if their children are cheerful and appear to be happy, they have done their job. This is the very time when, in a spirit of happiness and joy, the important lessons about life and God can be taught. This is the time when habits can be formed that will help young men and women resist the inevitable temptations that will come their way as they grow older. [20]

I wish that when I was a boy my father would have gathered us children up and read the Bible to us. I wish he would have prayed with us and taught us to sing as a family. I could have developed good habits and known where to start when I became a father in my early 20s. Family worship should be an extremely important part of your day. It should be something your children grow up thinking is a normal part of the Christian experience. Unfortunately, I did not begin my family this way and it has taken time to develop consistent family worship in our home. What I have learned over the years is that family worship, or Bible Time as we sometimes call it, does not have to be complicated. We just need to be consistent. I am inspired by the great preacher Charles Spurgeon, who despite leading an incredibly busy life, always made time for family worship.

> God gave Spurgeon an extraordinary capacity for work and productivity. And yet, despite the ceaseless, crushing demands on his schedule, at 6:00 each evening, setting aside a to-do list that few could match today, he gathered his wife, twin boys, and all others present in his home at the time for family worship. [21]

How Do You Do Family Worship?

I have been asked this question more than once. Fortunately, I have a very simple answer. All you have to do is read, pray, and sing. Voddie Baucham gives one of the best descriptions of family worship that I am aware of:

> Family worship isn't a full-on church service

> every day; instead it's a brief time of devotion before the Lord. The elements are singing, Scripture reading, and prayer. That's it! You sing together, pray together, and read the Scriptures together. Giving fifteen to twenty minutes a day to these simple practices will transform your family. [22]

That really is just it! If fact, reading Voddie Baucham's book *Family Shepherds* was a major turning point in our family worship.

I struggled for years to be consistent in our Bible Time. Sometimes it was better than others, but often I forgot about it or got busy with other things. It was on a business trip to Singapore that I read the words I quoted above and realized 1) I must do this; 2) I can do this. I was so encouraged I began family worship right away from my hotel room in Singapore through my iPad. It wasn't that easy with the latency, but we sang, we prayed, and we read the Bible. Today, family worship is one of my favorite times I spend with my children.

Tailor Family Worship to Your Life and Family

Family worship does not look the same every day. My favorite time is on Saturday morning or when I have Fridays off. I typically get up and make pancakes or waffles. After everyone is done we gather in the living room to begin our family worship time. It typically goes like this. We will pray and ask God's blessings on our time together. Next, we sing a few hymns. I play guitar, so I usually get that out. Through our AppleTV I will project the words of a song on our TV and we will all sing together. Sometimes I will start with children's songs like "Jesus Loves Me" or "This Little Light of Mine." Then I will play a hymn from one of the many hymnals we have in the house. We often sing the same song every time until we learn it well. After we sing a few songs, we read the Bible. We read through the Bible. Typically, one or two chapters. I keep a particular Bible on the shelf in our living room that I read from and mark so we remember where we are. The children also bring their Bibles and I will have several of them read a section. Even a beginning reader will get to read a sentence or two. This helps them all to be engaged. I sometimes explain what we have read, but often it is good enough to let the Word of God stand as is. Finally, we pray again. I take prayer requests and we talk about things we need to be praying for. Once the final prayer is through we sing the Doxology.

While singing, praying, and Scripture reading are the priority, I sometimes bring other elements into our family worship. On Saturday morning, I normally will read from a book. I have read things like *Foxe's Book of Martyrs* or other books that encourage us in the Lord. I have also at times taught catechism to the children during our family worship. There are a number of great catechisms out there. We typically use "A Catechism for Girls and Boys." It is found online at www.reformedreader.org/ccc/acbg.htm. There are other catechisms you can find which will come from your denominational perspective. I like this one because it is easy to memorize and understand.

During the week our family worship often takes on a different style. I am at work all day and our evenings are busy with seven children. Often, we will have family devotions at the dinner table while we are eating together. I may read from a devotion book that includes Scripture. We typically only sing one song and pray at the end of our time together. It is not uncommon for me to be exhausted. Having something like the *Psalms Study Guide* from Generations is a great way to read the Scripture but read someone else's explanation when it may be difficult for my tired brain to think of something to say. Other times during the week I may notice that my wife is having a tough time getting dinner together or there may be a lot of chaos going on. At these times I gather the children in the living room before dinner and we have family worship while she is finishing preparing dinner. Since our living room is connected to the kitchen my wife is able to hear what we are discussing.

Training for Church

My wife and I came to the conclusion that church was meant for the entire family. All of our children attend the worship service on Sunday together. We are sometimes asked, "How do you teach your children to sit through an 'adult' service?" My response is simply that they have been doing it all week at home. Having family worship is great practice for children to learn how to sit still through a church service or any other activity that requires them to sit for a while. It is much easier to deal with behavior issues in the privacy of your home than in a public setting. We still have a 2- and a 4-year-old. They do not always want to sit still and listen. Whenever we are having family worship, if one of the children will not sit still or be quiet, I simply take them out of the room. I explain to them why they need to sit and listen, and I lovingly discipline them. Then we head back to the living room and continue with our family devotions. If you are consistent, they will eventually understand that they need to sit and be quiet during family worship, and that will translate into sitting quietly for church.

You may challenge me on this and tell me that I do not know your children. You may say they will not sit and listen no matter what you do. I understand that it can be challenging, and sometimes extremely frustrating. However, as fathers, we need to be in control of our families. In First Timothy,

Paul gives qualifications for elders and deacons. **"He must manage his own household well, with all dignity keeping his children submissive"** (1 Timothy 3:4). While Paul is specifically addressing elders and deacons, all men should take this as instruction. I know it is difficult but ask God for wisdom and seek to be consistent. Rely on the Holy Spirit to give you self-control, and discipline consistently in love with humility. If you have had trouble with anger, ask your family for forgiveness. A helpful book for dealing with behavior issues is *Pitchin' A Fit!: Overcoming Angry and Stressed-Out Parenting* by Israel and Brook Wayne. You can find many other great parenting resources at their website, www.familyrenewal.org.

As a final reminder, family worship does not have to be complicated. It does not have to take a long time. Remember to sing, pray, read the Scriptures, and be consistent. Try to do it every day. It is not always possible in our home, but whenever we are together we make an effort to be consistent. I like to make it happen even when I am not home by utilizing today's technology. It is extremely important to exercise your God-given leadership as an ordinary homeschool dad, to lead your family spiritually. Having a consistent family worship is a great place to start, and your family will benefit tremendously from it.

Important Things to Teach Your Children

While I believe it is extremely important to have a routine family worship time, training your children to be Christ-honoring men and women involves training them throughout the day even in the mundane. This is the imperative of Deuteronomy 6. Every academic subject can be used to build a Biblical worldview in our children. My wife, Ruth Adams, states this beautifully:

> I am furthermore grateful that I have the freedom to educate my own children at home where we are learning that history is His Story, that science proclaims the works of a wonderful Creator, that music is a way we can glorify our Lord, that reading enables us to read the very words of God, and so forth. In all of our studies, we are trying to paint a picture of divine providence and the sovereignty of God. We are trying to instill a Biblical worldview so that our children can see all of life through the lens of God, His Word, and His ways. [5, p. 193]

While I do my best to have intentional family worship each day, my wife spends much more time with our children. This is a typical scenario for ordinary homeschool dads. I described in a previous chapter how we divvy up the academics. Additionally, my wife has a very special time with all the children which she calls their "circle time." This is the time she gathers all the children together in the living room and goes through an assortment of different topics. She will read to them on Biblical worldview, history, hymns and music, and even review math facts. It is a special time where they will sing, pray, laugh, and have deep discussions about Scripture and the ways of the Lord. It brings me great joy to hear from my children what they did in circle time.

Over the years my wife and I have narrowed what we believe are the most important things to teach our children before they leave home. It is not the academics. I am not saying we should neglect academics, but it is not the most important thing. Saint Irenaeus said it well. "It's better and brings greater benefit, to be a simple, uneducated man or woman, and to become akin to God through love, than to be well-read and clever (in our own conceited opinion) and to blaspheme the God who made us, by making up some imaginary God and Father of our own." [13, p. Feb 24] We honestly would rather our children come to know, love, and fear Jesus Christ than to have an Ivy League education.

In her book, *Legacy*, my wife listed those items we believe are most important and I want to briefly summarize them here. You will notice a common theme with much of what I have already written

1. **The Gospel**—The good news that, though

we are born dead in sin, God has provided a means of forgiveness of sin through the finished work of Jesus Christ on the cross, that through repentance and faith in Him we are made right with God and will receive the gift of eternity with Him when our life on earth is over. **"For by grace you have been saved through faith. And this is not your own doing; it is the gift of God, not a result of works, so that no one may boast"** (Ephesians 2:8-9).

2. **Ongoing Repentance**—Martin Luther said it well in the first article of his *95 Theses*. "When our Lord and Master Jesus Christ said, `Repent' (Matt. 4:17), he willed the entire life of believers to be one of repentance." **"Repent therefore, and turn back, that your sins may be blotted out"** (Acts 3:19).

3. **Prayer**—We want our children to have prayer as their first action instead of a last resort. 1 Thessalonians 5:16-18 says to **"pray without ceasing."**

4. **Cherish, Trust and Defend the Word of God**—**"All Scripture is breathed out by God and profitable for teaching, for reproof, for correction, and for training in righteousness, that the man of God may be complete, equipped for every good work"** (1 Timothy 3:16-17).

5. **Church History**—Seeing the providence of God played out in history builds our faith and helps us to trust God for our future. **"The Lord brings the counsel of the nations to nothing; he frustrates the plans of the peoples"** (Psalm 33:10).

6. **Sound Doctrine**—**"So that we may no longer be children, tossed to and fro by the waves and carried about by every wind of doctrine, by human cunning, by craftiness in deceitful schemes"** (Ephesians 4:14).

7. **To Memorize God's Word**—**"Thy word have I hid in mine heart, that I might not sin against thee"** (Psalm 119:11, KJV).

8. **The Honor of Suffering for Christ**— Reading *Foxe's Book of Martyrs* or other works on Christian persecution will help our children to understand what a privilege it is to live in a free country and to not take those freedoms for granted. It will prepare them to stand firm if they are ever faced with hostility towards their faith. **"Indeed, all who desire to live a godly life in Christ Jesus will be persecuted"** (2 Timothy 3:12).

9. **Obedience**—Learning to obey and respect authority is extremely important for their health and wellbeing. We live in a culture that more and more disrespects authority and prides itself in rebellion. Ultimately, they must learn they are accountable to God for their actions. **"Children, obey your parents**

in the Lord, for this is right" (Ephesians 6:1).

10. **Good Character**—If our children learn character qualities such as trustworthiness, honesty, hard work, deference, humility, modesty, and politeness out of a love for Christ Jesus, their opportunity for success will be greatly increased. **"Even a child makes himself known by his acts, by whether his conduct is pure and upright"** (Proverbs 20:11).

11. **The Importance of Serving**—We live in a very self-centered culture. Some call it the "selfie generation." When children are taught to serve and given opportunities to help other people they begin to realize how fortunate they are. It is amazing how young faces will light up when they know they have done something to help another person. **"Do not neglect to do good and to share what you have, for such sacrifices are pleasing to God"** (Hebrews 13:16).

12. **Gratitude**—Being thankful and showing appreciation is pleasing to God. After all, everything we have is a gift from God and because we are sinful people we do not deserve any good thing. When we are thankful we are less likely to be depressed but will have more joy. The Bible says that it is God's will for us to be thankful. **"Give thanks in all circumstances; for this is the**

will of God in Christ Jesus for you" (1 Thessalonians 5:18).

13. **God-Honoring Music**—We love to sing hymns in our family. Hymns are timeless and connect us with the saints of old. They often carry deep theological truths that point us to God. We are also told to sing in Scripture and it is not just to be an emotional experience. **"I will sing praise with my spirit, but I will sing with my mind also"** (1 Corinthians 14:15). **"Let the word of Christ dwell in you richly, teaching and admonishing one another in all wisdom, singing psalms and hymns and spiritual songs, with thankfulness in your hearts to God"** (Colossians 3:16).

These are the things that are important to us for our children. This is what constitutes success in our homeschool and are things that can be taught throughout each day. The Scripture reference I included with each principle is there not only to demonstrate the Biblical foundation for why we want to teach these things, but as an example to always let our children know why we do what we do in our homeschool. Towards the end of Deuteronomy 6, God told the children of Israel why He gave them the rules and laws that they were to follow. **"When your son asks you in time to come, 'What is the meaning of the testimonies and the statutes and the rules that the Lord our God has commanded you?' then you shall say to your son, 'We were**

Pharaoh's slaves in Egypt. And the Lord brought us out of Egypt with a mighty hand"
(Deuteronomy 6:20-21). When children do not understand the direction your family is going, or the household rules your family lives by, they can become exasperated. As Christian fathers we do not want to provoke our children, as Ephesians 6:4 tells us. When we continually point them to the Bible for the reasons we live the way we do, they are better able to understand the "why" behind our instructions. Jesus Christ is that solid rock on which we stand and the firm foundation that our children need as they grow to be the men and women we pray for. His Word will stand forever. May the Lord bless you as you seek to train your children in the nurture and admonition of the Lord (Ephesians 6:4).

Conclusion

I can do all things through Christ who strengthens me (Philippians 4:13, NKJV).

Ordinary homeschool dad, I want to wrap this book up by way of encouragement that you can do this. I have written this book on my lunch break at the office, on airplanes, and in hotel rooms while on business trips. I am just another ordinary guy like you, trying to lead my homeschooling family. We don't have to be professional speakers, authors, curriculum producers, or even pastors, elders, or deacons. We just need to be faithful to do what God has called us to do through Christ Jesus our Savior.

Use the book summary below as a reminder.

1. **Pray.** Pray for your family and pray with your family. **"Confess your trespasses to one another, and pray for one another, that you may be healed. The effective, fervent prayer of a righteous man avails much"** (James 5:16, NKJV).
2. **Support your wife.** Find out where she needs help. Take the load off her and love her. **"Husbands, love your wives, just as Christ also loved the church and gave Himself for her"** (Ephesians 5:25, NKJV).

3. **Go places.** Go to conferences that encourage you in your faith and learn history as you go. **"And these words that I command you today shall be on your heart. You shall teach them diligently to your children, and shall talk of them when you sit in your house, and when you walk by the way, and when you lie down, and when you rise"** (Deuteronomy 6:6-7).

4. **Defend the faith.** Teach your children that they can trust the Bible. Teach them Church history. Teach them Biblical creation. Teach them to defend these things when challenged and teach them that there are good answers even if they do not immediately know them. **"But in your hearts honor Christ the Lord as holy, always being prepared to make a defense to anyone who asks you for a reason for the hope that is in you; yet do it with gentleness and respect"** (1 Peter 3:15).

5. **Have family worship.** Sing, pray, and read the Bible, and do it as consistently as you can. **"Therefore let us be grateful for receiving a kingdom that cannot be shaken, and thus let us offer to God acceptable worship, with reverence and awe, for our God is a consuming fire"** (Hebrews 12:28-29).

That's it, guys. My prayer is that this book has encouraged you and motivated you to live out your faith in your home as an ordinary man. I will be praying for you, homeschool dad. Please pray for me. It's a tough job being an ordinary homeschool dad, and I don't always measure up. By God's grace we can do this together and *may God give the increase* (1 Corinthians 3:7).

Be watchful, stand firm in the faith, act like men, be strong (1 Corinthians 16:13).

Resource List

All Scripture is breathed out by God and profitable for teaching, for reproof, for correction, and for training in righteousness, that the man of God may be complete, equipped for every good work (2 Timothy 3:16-17).

While Scripture is our final authority, the following books have been useful to me in becoming a better husband, father, and defender of the faith. It is not an exhaustive list. There are other books not in my reference list that you may want to consider. Most of these authors have written many other books on specific topics that would be helpful as you equip yourself to become better at being an ordinary homeschool dad.

Family

1. *Family Shepherds: Calling and Equipping Men to Lead Their Homes*—Voddie Baucham Jr.
2. *The Masculine Mandate: God's Calling to Men*—Richard D. Phillips
3. *Pitchin' A Fit!: Overcoming Angry and Stressed-Out Parenting*—Israel & Brook Wayne
4. *Full-Time Parenting: A Guide to Family-Based Discipleship*—Israel Wayne
5. *Answers for Homeschooling*—Israel Wayne

6. *Strong Fathers, Strong Daughters: 10 Secrets Every Father Should Know*—Meg Meeker
7. *Bringing Up Boys: Practical Advice and Encouragement for Those Shaping the Next Generation Of Men*—James Dobson

Apologetics

1. *Defending Your Faith: An Introduction to Apologetics*—R. C. Sproul
2. *The Case for Christ: A Journalist's Personal Investigation of the Evidence for Jesus*—Lee Strobel
3. *Christian Apologetics*—Cornelius Van Til

Defending The Bible

4. *Scripture Alone: Exploring the Bible's Accuracy, Authority and Authenticity*—James R. White
5. *The King James Only Controversy: Can You Trust Modern Translations?*—James R. White
6. *Canon Revisited: Establishing the Origins and Authority of the New Testament Books*—Michael J. Kruger
7. *Understanding Genesis: How to Analyze, Interpret, and Defend Scripture*—Jason Lisle
8. *Keeping Faith in an Age of Reason: Refuting Alleged Bible Contradictions*—Jason Lisle
9. *New International Encyclopedia of Bible Difficulties*—Gleason L. Archer Jr.

Defending Biblical Creation

10. *Ultimate Proof of Creation*—Jason Lisle
11. *The Evolution of a Creationist: A Layman's Guide to the Conflict Between the Bible and Evolutionary Theory*—Jobe Martin

12. *Bones of Contention: A Creationist Assessment of Human Fossils*—Marvin L. Lubenow
13. *Replacing Darwin: The New Origin of Species*—Nathaniel T Jeanson

Church History/Culture

14. *Daily Readings: The Early Church Fathers*—Nick Needham
15. *2,000 Years of Christ's Power* (Vol. 1, 2, 3, & 4)—Nick Needham
16. *Apostate: The Men Who Destroyed the Christian West*—Kevin Swanson
17. *Education: Does God Have an Opinion?*—Israel Wayne

MATTHEW D. ADAMS

References

[1] John W. Yates, *How a Man Prays for His Family* (Little Rock, Arkansas: FamilyLife, 2004), p. 58.

[2] Todd Wilson, *Help! I'm Married to a Homeschooling Mom* (Chicago: Moody Publishers, 2004), pp. 79-80.

[3] Lance C. Wubbels, *The Power of Prayer in a Believer's Life* (Lynnwood, Washington: Emerald Books, 1993), p. 17.

[4] Richard D. Phillips, *The Masculine Mandate: God's Calling to Men* (Sanford, Florida: Reformation Trust Publishing, 2010), p. 87.

[5] Ruth L. Adams, *Legacy: Reflections of a Homeschooled, Homeschooling Mama* (Hempstead, Texas: Ruth L. Adams, 2017), p. 134.

[6] Ken Ham, B. Beemer and T. Hillard, *Already Gone: Why your kids will quit church and what you can do to stop it* (Green Forest, Arkansas: Master Books, 2009), p. 24. (It won't let me create a sidebar comment on footnotes. Is this subheader capitalized?)

[7] R. C. Sproul, *Defending Your Faith: An Introduction to Apologetics* (Wheaton, Illinois: Crossway Books, 2003), p. 13.

[8] Cornelius Van Til, *Christian Apologetics* (Phillipsburg, New Jersey: P&R Publishing Company, 2003), p. 1.

[9] Lee Strobel, *The Case for Christ: A Journalist's Personal Investigation of the Evidence for Jesus* (Grand Rapids,

Michigan: Zondervan, 1998), p. 266.

[10] Jason Lisle, *Ultimate Proof of Creation* (Green Forest, Arkansas: Master Books, 2009), p. 52.

[11] James R. White, *The King James Only Controversy: Can You Trust Modern Translations?* (Bloomington, Minnesota: Bethany House Publishers, 2009), p. 63.

[12] Nick Needham, *2,000 Years of Christ's Power Vol. 1: The Age of the Early Church Fathers* (London: Grace Publications, 2016), p. 106.

[13] Nick Needham, *Daily Readings—the Early Church Fathers* (Ross-shire, Scotland: Christian Focus Publications, 2017).

[14] M. R. James, "Gnosis.org," The Gnostic Society Library, 1924. Available: http://gnosis.org/library/inftoma.htm. [Accessed 9 May 2018.]

[15] Michael J. Kruger, *Canon Revisited: Establishing the Origins and Authority of the New Testament Books* (Wheaton, Illinois: Crossway, 2012), pp. 200-201.

[16] Jason Lisle, *Keeping Faith in an Age of Reason: Refuting Alleged Bible Contradictions* (Green Forest, Arkansas: Master Books, 2017), p. 8.

[17] Jobe Martin, *The Evolution Of A Creationist*, (2013), p. 135.

[18] Richard Lewontin, "The New York Review of Books," NYREV, Inc., 9 January 1997. Available: http://www.nybooks.com/articles/1997/01/09/billions-and-billions-of-demons. [Accessed 9 May 2018.]

[19] Nathaniel T. Jeanson, *Replacing Darwin: The New Origin of Species*, 180 ed. (Green Forest, Arkansas: Master Books, 2017).

[20] William Wilberforce, *Real Christianity* (Ventura, California: Regal Books, 2006), pp. 170-171.

[21] Don Whitney, "Too busy to lead family worship?," The Center for Biblical Spirituality, 11 November 2014. Available: http://biblicalspirituality.org/too-busy-to-lead-family-worship. [Accessed 9 May 2018.]

[22] Voddie Baucham Jr., *Family Shepherds: Calling and Equipping Men to Lead Their Homes* (Wheaton, Illinois: Crossway, 2011), p. 79.

Made in the USA
Columbia, SC
03 May 2022